FINANCIAL LITERACY AND MONEY SKILLS FOR TWEENS

Empowering the Next Generation to Make Smart Money Choices

By
ELIZABETH BILL

Copyright © 2024 by ELIZABETH BILL

All rights reserved. No part of this publication may be reproduced, distributed, or transmitted in any form or by any means, including photocopying, recording, or other electronic or mechanical methods, without the prior written permission of the publisher, except in the case of brief quotations embodied in critical reviews and certain other noncommercial uses permitted by copyright law.

This publication is designed to provide accurate and authoritative information in regard to the subject matter covered. It is sold with the understanding that the publisher is not engaged in rendering legal, accounting, or other professional advice. If legal advice or other expert assistance is required, the services of a competent professional person should be sought.

DEDICATION

To the next generation of financial wizards—may you navigate the world of money with confidence, wisdom, and a heart full of generosity. This book is dedicated to all the young minds ready to take charge of their financial future.

To my family and friends, whose support and encouragement continue to inspire me every day.

And to every parent, guardian, and mentor guiding the youth toward a brighter financial future—your efforts make all the difference.

TABLE OF CONTENTS

DEDICATION   3

INTRODUCTION   9

CHAPTER ONE   12

   UNDERSTANDING MONEY -------- 12

      What is money?   12

      A brief history of money   12

   THE DIFFERENT FORMS OF MONEY -------- 13

      Physical Money: Cash and Coins   13

      Digital Money: Debit Cards, Mobile Payments, and Cryptocurrencies   13

   THE ROLE OF MONEY IN SOCIETY -------- 15

CHAPTER TWO   17

   EARNING MONEY AS A TWEEN -------- 17

      Why Earning Money Matters   17

      Creative Ways to Earn Money   19

      Learning to Value Your Time and Effort   22

      Setting Goals for Your Earnings   22

   THE IMPORTANCE OF A GROWTH MINDSET -------- 23

   Going Digital: Earning Money Online -------- 27

   Balancing School and Earning Money -------- 29

   CHAPTER THREE -------- 30

   MANAGING AND BUDGETING YOUR MONEY -------- 30

      The Importance of Needs vs. Wants   34

      Smart Spending Tips   35

CHAPTER FOUR 37

THE POWER OF SAVING MONEY   37

    Why Saving Matters   37

    How to Develop a Saving Habit   38

    Different Types of Savings   39

CHAPTER 5 43

UNDERSTANDING CREDIT AND DEBT ------------------------------------ 43

    Understanding Credit and Debt   43

    What Is Credit?   43

    Types of Credit: 43

    What Is Debt?   44

    What Is a Credit Score?   46

    How Your Credit Score Is Calculated: 46

    Smart Ways to Avoid Debt   47

CHAPTER 6 -- 49

SMART SPENDING HABITS   49

    Why Smart Spending Matters   49

    Steps to Create a Spending Plan: 51

    Tips to Avoid Impulse Buying: 52

CHAPTER 7 -- 56

THE BASICS OF INVESTING   56

    What Is Investing?   56

    How Investing Works   56

    Why Invest?   58

    Risk and Reward: The Balance of Investing   59

How to Get Started With Investing 59

CHAPTER 8 ----- 63

CHOOSING THE RIGHT INVESTMENTS 63

What's Your Investment Goal? 63

Risk Tolerance: How Much Can You Handle? 64

Types of Investment Strategies 65

Diversification: Don't Put All Your Eggs in One Basket 66

CHAPTER 9 ----- 70

AVOIDING COMMON INVESTMENT MISTAKES 70

CHAPTER 10 ----- 78

TRACKING YOUR PROGRESS AND STAYING MOTIVATED 78

Why Tracking Your Progress Matters ----- 78

Benefits of Tracking Your Progress: 78

How to Track Your Financial Goals 78

The power of consistency 82

CHAPTER 11 ----- 84

THE POWER OF COMPOUND INTEREST 84

What Is Compound Interest? 84

How Compound Interest Works: 84

Why Compound Interest Is Powerful 85

The "Time" Factor: 85

How to Maximize the Power of Compound Interest 86

CHAPTER 12 ----- 89

Budgeting for Tweens – Planning Your Money Wisely 89

What Is a Budget? ----- 89

Why You Need a Budget:	89
How to Create a Simple Budget	90
How Budgeting Helps You Reach Your Goals	92

CHAPTER 13 94

EARNING MONEY AS A TWEEN – START BUILDING YOUR OWN INCOME ... 94

Why Earning Money as a Tween Is Important	94
Ways to Earn Money as a Tween	95
Turning Your Skills into Income	97
Things to Remember When Earning Money	98

CHAPTER 14 100

SAVING AND INVESTING – GROWING YOUR MONEY FOR THE FUTURE ... 100

What Is Saving? 100

Why Is Saving Important?	100
Tips for Saving Money	101
What Is Investing?	101
Types of Investments for Beginners	102
How to Start Investing as a Tween	104

CONCLUSION **107**

INTRODUCTION

Welcome to **"Financial Literacy and Money Skills for Tweens: Empowering the Next Generation to Make Smart Money Choices."** This book is your guide to understanding the world of money—a world that might seem complicated at first but is actually full of exciting opportunities.

Whether you're saving up for something special, thinking about starting a small business, or just curious about how money works, this book is here to help you navigate it all. Money is a powerful tool, and when you learn how to use it wisely, you can achieve your dreams and help others along the way.

Why This Book Matters

As you grow up, you'll find that money plays a big role in almost every part of life. From buying snacks at the store to saving for college or a new gadget, making smart money choices is essential. But here's the thing—many people don't learn about money until they're much older, and sometimes, they miss out on important lessons that could have helped them avoid mistakes.

This book is different. It's designed just for you—a tween who's ready to take control of their financial future. You're at the perfect age to start building good money habits that will serve you for the rest of your life. By understanding the basics of earning, saving, spending, and investing, you'll be setting yourself up for success.

What You'll Learn

Throughout this book, we'll cover a wide range of topics, from how to create a budget and save for big goals, to the ins and outs of investing and even starting your own business. You'll learn how to distinguish between needs and wants, how to avoid falling into debt, and how to make money work for you.

Each chapter is packed with practical tips, real-life examples, and fun activities that will help you apply what you learn. You'll also find stories of young people just like you who have taken control of their finances and achieved amazing things.

How to Use This Book

Feel free to read this book from start to finish, or jump to the chapters that interest you the most. Each chapter builds on the last, but you can always come back and revisit sections as you start applying these skills in real life.

There are also questions and activities at the end of each chapter designed to help you think about how the concepts apply to your own life. Don't be afraid to take your time with these exercises—this is your journey, and it's important to go at your own pace.

A Journey Toward Financial Independence

By the time you finish this book, you'll have a solid understanding of money and the confidence to make smart financial decisions. You'll be on your way to becoming financially independent, capable of managing your money wisely, and ready to face the challenges and opportunities that life brings.

Remember, the habits you build now will stick with you for a lifetime. So let's get started on this exciting journey together. Your future is bright, and with the right tools and knowledge, there's no limit to what you can achieve.

CHAPTER ONE

UNDERSTANDING MONEY

Money is a big part of our lives, but have you ever stopped to think about what money really is? This chapter will take you on a journey to explore the basics of money—what it is, why we use it, and how it shapes the world around us. By the end, you'll have a solid understanding of the foundation of financial literacy.

What is money?

At its core, money is a medium of exchange. This means it's something people use to trade for goods and services. Instead of swapping items directly, like trading a toy for a book, money allows you to buy the book outright. You can think of money as a tool that makes trading easier.

Money can come in many forms. The most common types you've probably seen are cash (paper bills) and coins, but money also includes things like debit cards, checks, and even digital currencies. The key thing to remember is that money is only valuable because everyone agrees that it is. It's a shared belief in its value that keeps the system running.

A brief history of money

Money hasn't always looked the way it does today. Thousands of years ago, people didn't have coins or bills—they traded goods directly in a system known as bartering. For example, if someone had extra grain and needed some tools, they would trade their grain for the tools with someone who had them. But this system wasn't always convenient. What if the person with the tools didn't need grain? This is where the idea of money came in.

Over time, people started using items like shells, beads, and metals as money because these were easier to trade. Eventually, coins made from precious metals like gold and silver became popular because they were durable and had intrinsic value (value in themselves). As societies grew more complex, paper money was introduced as a way to make large transactions easier, and today, we also use digital money that exists only in computers and phones.

THE DIFFERENT FORMS OF MONEY

Today, money comes in several different forms, each with its own uses and characteristics. Let's explore some of the most common ones.

Physical Money: Cash and Coins

When you think of money, you probably picture cash—paper bills like dollars, euros, or pounds—and coins. These are the physical forms of money that you can hold in your hand. Each bill and coin has a specific value, and together, they make up the currency used in your country.

Cash is great for everyday purchases, like buying snacks or paying for a bus ride. Coins are often used for smaller transactions, while paper bills are used for larger amounts. But carrying a lot of cash can be inconvenient, especially for big purchases, which is where other forms of money come in.

Digital Money: Debit Cards, Mobile Payments, and Cryptocurrencies

In today's world, a lot of money exists digitally. Instead of carrying cash, many people use debit cards, credit cards, or mobile payment apps like Apple Pay or Google Wallet. These forms of money are stored electronically in bank accounts and can be accessed instantly when you need to make a purchase.

Debit Cards: These are linked directly to your bank account. When you use a debit card to buy something, the money is taken out of your account immediately. Debit cards are great because they're easy to use and you don't have to carry cash, but it's important to keep track of your spending to avoid overdrawing your account.

Credit Cards: While similar to debit cards, credit cards work a bit differently. When you use a credit card, you're borrowing money from the bank that you'll need to pay back later. If you pay your balance in full each month, you won't be charged interest, but if you don't, the bank will charge you extra for borrowing the money over time. Credit cards can be useful, but they require careful management.

Mobile Payments: These are digital wallets stored on your smartphone. You can link your debit or credit card to a mobile payment app and use your phone to pay for things. This is becoming more common in stores and online because it's fast and convenient.

Cryptocurrencies: These are a new form of digital money that exists only online, like Bitcoin or Ethereum. Unlike traditional money, cryptocurrencies aren't controlled by any government or bank. They use complex technology called blockchain to keep track of transactions.

While they're still new and can be risky, some people believe they represent the future of money.

THE ROLE OF MONEY IN SOCIETY

Money does more than just help you buy things—it plays a crucial role in society. Let's explore some of the ways money impacts the world around us.

Facilitating Trade and Business

One of the main reasons money exists is to make trade easier. Without money, it would be challenging to exchange goods and services. Imagine trying to run a business where you had to barter for everything you needed—finding someone who has what you want and wants what you have would be difficult and time-consuming.

With money, you can buy what you need from anyone, and they can do the same. This makes it possible for businesses to grow and for economies to function smoothly. Whether it's a small store in your neighborhood or a massive company that sells products worldwide, money is what keeps trade flowing.

Enabling Investment and Growth

Money also allows people and businesses to invest in the future. When you save money, you can use it later to achieve a goal, like buying a car, starting a business, or going to college. Businesses can invest money to expand, create new products, and hire more employees, which helps the economy grow.

Investments can take many forms, from putting money in a savings account to buying stocks or real estate. The idea is to use money to create more value over time, which benefits both individuals and society as a whole.

Supporting Government and Public Services

Governments collect money through taxes to fund public services like schools, hospitals, roads, and parks. Taxes are payments that citizens make to the government based on things like income, property, and purchases. Without taxes, governments wouldn't be able to provide these essential services that help everyone.

In addition to funding public services, money allows governments to stabilize the economy. For example, during times of economic crisis, governments can use money to support businesses and individuals, helping the economy recover more quickly.

The Power of Money

Money might seem like just a bunch of coins, bills, and numbers, but it's actually one of the most powerful tools we have. It shapes our lives in countless ways, from the simple act of buying a snack to the complex systems that drive the global economy. Understanding money is the first step toward using it wisely.

As you continue reading this book, you'll learn how to manage money, make smart financial decisions, and even use money to achieve your goals. Remember, money itself isn't good or bad—it's how you use it that matters. With the right knowledge and habits, you can make money work for you, opening up a world of possibilities.

CHAPTER TWO

EARNING MONEY AS A TWEEN

Now that you understand what money is and how it works, it's time to talk about one of the most exciting parts—earning your own money! Having your own money gives you the freedom to buy things you want, save for future goals, and even help others. In this chapter, we'll explore different ways you can start earning money as a tween, from small jobs to creative business ideas.

Why Earning Money Matters

Earning your own money is more than just about having cash in your pocket. It teaches you valuable life skills like responsibility, time management, and the value of hard work. When you earn money, you learn to appreciate it more, and you become more careful about how you spend it. It's also the first step toward financial independence—something that will benefit you for the rest of your life.

Small Jobs You Can Do

Even if you're not old enough for a part-time job, there are plenty of small jobs you can do to start earning money. Here are some ideas:

1. Chores Around the House

One of the easiest ways to earn money is by doing extra chores at home. Many parents are willing to pay for tasks like washing the car, mowing the lawn, cleaning the garage, or helping with household organization.

Talk to your parents about what needs to be done and agree on a fair payment.

How to Get Started: Make a list of chores that need to be done and discuss them with your parents. Set a price for each task and create a schedule that works for everyone.

2. Pet Sitting and Dog Walking

If you love animals, pet sitting and dog walking can be a fun way to earn money. Many people need someone to take care of their pets when they're away, and they're willing to pay for it. Dog walking is another great option, especially if your neighbors are busy and need help exercising their pets.

How to Get Started: Let your neighbors know that you're available for pet sitting or dog walking. You can create flyers to advertise your services or ask your parents to help you spread the word on social media.

3. Babysitting

Babysitting is a popular way for tweens to earn money. If you're responsible and enjoy spending time with younger kids, this could be a great option for you. You can start by babysitting for family members or close friends and gradually expand as you gain experience.

How to Get Started: Take a babysitting course to learn the basics of childcare and first aid. Once you're certified, let people in your community know that you're available for babysitting.

4. Tutoring

If you're good at a particular subject, you can offer tutoring services to younger kids who need help with their schoolwork. Whether it's math, reading, or science, tutoring is a great way to use your knowledge to earn money while helping others.

How to Get Started: Offer your tutoring services to neighbors, family friends, or classmates. You can also create flyers or ask your teacher to help you find students who need tutoring.

5. Yard Work

In addition to mowing lawns, you can offer to rake leaves, shovel snow, or plant flowers for your neighbors. Yard work is a seasonal job that can keep you busy throughout the year, depending on where you live.

How to Get Started: Walk around your neighborhood and offer your services to people who need help with their yards. You can charge by the hour or by the task, depending on what's needed.

Creative Ways to Earn Money

If you're more entrepreneurial and enjoy being creative, there are many other ways to earn money that allow you to showcase your talents and interests.

1. Selling Handmade Crafts

If you're good at making things like jewelry, candles, or artwork, you can sell your handmade crafts to earn money. Many people appreciate unique, handmade items, and you can sell them at local craft fairs, online, or to friends and family.

How to Get Started: Decide what you want to make and start creating a small inventory. Once you have enough items, set up an online store using platforms like Etsy, or sell at local markets and fairs.

2. Starting a YouTube Channel or Blog

If you enjoy creating content, starting a YouTube channel or blog can be a fun way to earn money. You can create videos or write about topics you're passionate about, whether it's gaming, cooking, DIY projects, or fashion. Over time, as your audience grows, you can earn money through ads, sponsorships, and merchandise sales.

How to Get Started: Choose a topic you're interested in and start creating content. Be consistent and engage with your audience. Once your channel or blog gains traction, explore ways to monetize it.

3. Designing and Selling T-Shirts

If you have an eye for design, you can create your own T-shirt designs and sell them online. Platforms like Teespring and Redbubble allow you to upload your designs, and they handle the printing and shipping for you.

How to Get Started: Use free design tools like Canva to create your T-shirt designs. Upload them to an online platform and start promoting your store to friends, family, and on social media.

4. Creating and Selling Digital Products

Digital products like eBooks, printables, and digital art can be sold online with minimal cost. If you enjoy writing, designing, or creating digital content, this could be a great way to earn money.

How to Get Started: Create your digital product using tools like Microsoft Word, Photoshop, or Canva. Once your product is ready, sell it on platforms like Gumroad, Etsy, or your own website.

5. Offering Tech Help

If you're tech-savvy, you can offer tech help to people in your community. This could include helping someone set up a new device, teaching them how to use software, or fixing minor computer problems.

How to Get Started: Let people know about your tech skills and offer your services for a small fee. You can also create a flyer or website to promote your tech help business.

Learning to Value Your Time and Effort

As you start earning money, it's important to learn the value of your time and effort. Not all jobs are the same, and some might take more time or skill than others. When deciding how much to charge for your services, think about how long the job will take and how difficult it is. Don't be afraid to negotiate a fair price for your work—your time and skills are valuable.

Setting Goals for Your Earnings

Once you start earning money, it's a good idea to set goals for what you want to do with it. Maybe you're saving for a new video game, a bike, or even donating to a charity you care about. Setting goals helps you stay focused and motivated, and it gives your earnings a purpose.

Short-Term Goals: These are things you want to achieve soon, like buying something small or saving for a trip. Short-term goals usually take a few weeks or months to reach.

Long-Term Goals: These are bigger goals that might take a year or more to achieve, like saving for a new computer or a big trip. Long-term goals require patience and dedication, but they're worth it.

Earning your own money as a tween is an exciting step toward financial independence. Whether you're doing small jobs, starting a business, or exploring creative ways to earn, you're learning important skills that will benefit you throughout your life. Remember, every dollar you earn is a result of your hard work, and with the right mindset and goals, you can achieve amazing things.

THE IMPORTANCE OF A GROWTH MINDSET

Before diving deeper into the ways you can earn money, it's important to adopt the right mindset. The growth mindset is the belief that abilities and intelligence can be developed through dedication and hard work. When it comes to earning money, having a growth mindset means being open to learning new skills, taking on challenges, and improving over time.

A tween with a growth mindset is always on the lookout for new opportunities to earn, learn, and grow. Instead of saying, "I can't do that," you should think, "How can I learn to do that?" Whether you're babysitting for the first time or starting a small business, every experience helps you grow.

More Small Jobs You Can Do

In addition to the jobs already mentioned, there are plenty of other opportunities for tweens to earn money in your community or even online.

1. Washing Cars

Car washing is a job that's always in demand. People love having clean cars but may not have the time to wash them. You can offer your services to family members, neighbors, or even advertise to a larger group. You'll need some basic supplies like soap, sponges, and buckets, which you may already have at home.

How to Get Started: Create a flyer offering your services or ask your neighbors directly if they need help washing their cars. You can also offer a deal where customers get a discount if they recommend you to their friends.

2. Organizing Garage Sales for Others

If you have a knack for organization and love helping people, you can offer to organize garage sales for your neighbors. Many people have items they no longer need, but setting up a garage sale can be overwhelming. You can help by pricing items, setting up displays, and managing the sale.

How to Get Started: Let your neighbors know that you can help organize their garage sales in exchange for a percentage of the earnings or a flat fee. You'll gain experience in organizing and managing money while helping others get rid of their clutter.

3. Delivering Newspapers

While fewer people receive paper newspapers today, there are still opportunities to work as a paper carrier. This is a traditional way for tweens to earn money by delivering newspapers to homes in the morning or afternoon.

How to Get Started: Check with your local newspaper to see if they are hiring delivery workers in your area. You can earn money and also develop responsibility by following a schedule.

4. Renting Out Your Stuff
Do you have items like bikes, video games, or tools that others might need but don't want to buy? You can rent them out for a small fee. This way, you're earning money without even having to sell anything!

How to Get Started: Make a list of items you're willing to rent out, and let your friends or neighbors know they can borrow them for a fee. Be sure to have clear rules about how long the item can be borrowed and what happens if it gets damaged.

Building Your Own Business
If you're ready to take things a step further, you can create your own small business. Building a business requires creativity, planning, and persistence, but it can be one of the most rewarding ways to earn money. Here are some business ideas that tweens can successfully start.

1. Lemonade Stand or Snack Stall
A classic way for tweens to earn money is by setting up a lemonade stand. On a hot day, people are more than happy to pay for a cold drink, and this simple business teaches you about marketing, customer service, and handling money.

How to Get Started: Set up a stand in your neighborhood or at a local event, and sell lemonade, cookies, or other snacks. Be sure to ask your parents for help in buying supplies and choosing a good location.

2. Gift Wrapping Service

During the holiday season or for birthdays, people often need help wrapping presents. If you're good at gift wrapping, you can offer your services to friends, family, or neighbors.

How to Get Started: Gather wrapping paper, scissors, tape, and ribbons, and offer to wrap gifts for a fee. You can also create custom gift-wrapping designs to attract more customers.

3. Custom Art and Illustrations

If you're artistic, you can turn your drawings into a business. Many people love custom artwork for birthdays, holidays, or home décor. You can sell your art online or at local fairs and events.

How to Get Started: Create a portfolio of your artwork and show it to potential customers. You can also take commissions where people pay you to create specific designs. Promote your work on social media or sell it through platforms like Etsy.

4. Homemade Baked Goods

Do you love baking cookies, cupcakes, or other treats? You can start a small baking business and sell your homemade goods to family and friends. Baking is a great way to combine your creativity with a profitable business idea.

How to Get Started: Test your recipes at home and ask for feedback from friends and family. Once you're confident in your baking skills, offer your treats at events, parties, or local fairs. Make sure to check with your parents about any local regulations for selling homemade food.

Going Digital: Earning Money Online

The internet offers endless opportunities for tweens to earn money online. While it's important to be careful and get permission from your parents, there are many legitimate ways to make money from home using your computer or smartphone.

1. Taking Online Surveys

Some websites pay people to take surveys and give their opinions on products and services. While you won't make a lot of money from surveys, it's an easy way to earn a little extra cash in your free time.

How to Get Started: Ask your parents to help you find legitimate survey websites that are safe for tweens. You'll answer questions about your preferences and experiences, and in return, you'll earn rewards or small payments.

2. Creating and Selling Digital Art

If you enjoy digital drawing or graphic design, you can create artwork that people can download and use for websites, social media, or personal projects. Platforms like Etsy allow you to sell digital downloads of your artwork, and once it's uploaded, you can earn money every time someone buys it.

How to Get Started: Use design software like Canva, Procreate, or Photoshop to create your digital art. Set up an online store where people can purchase and download your creations.

3. *Affiliate Marketing*

Affiliate marketing is when you promote products online and earn a commission when someone buys the product through your special link. If you have a blog, YouTube channel, or social media page, you can use affiliate marketing to recommend products you love and earn money when others buy them.

How to Get Started: Sign up for affiliate programs with companies that sell products you believe in. Share your affiliate links with your followers and make sure to explain why you recommend the product.

4. Selling Stock Photos

If you enjoy photography, you can sell your photos on stock photo websites. Companies and individuals often buy stock photos for their websites, ads, or social media, and you can earn money every time someone downloads your image.

How to Get Started: Take high-quality photos and upload them to stock photo websites like Shutterstock or Adobe Stock. Once your photos are approved, you'll start earning money every time they're downloaded.

Balancing School and Earning Money

As exciting as earning money can be, it's important to remember that school should always come first. Learning to balance your studies with earning money will teach you time management skills that will help you later in life. Here are some tips to maintain a healthy balance:

Set a Schedule: Make sure you have time for homework, hobbies, and relaxation. You can designate specific hours or days for your money-earning activities, so they don't interfere with your schoolwork.

Start Small: Begin with a manageable job or project, and as you get better at balancing your time, you can take on more tasks.

Ask for Help: If you find it hard to manage everything, ask your parents or a trusted adult for advice on how to balance your commitments.

By exploring small jobs, creative business ideas, and even digital opportunities, you're well on your way to becoming financially independent. Remember, every dollar you earn is a result of your hard work, creativity, and dedication. As you continue on this journey, don't forget to set financial goals, stay motivated, and always look for ways to improve and grow.

CHAPTER THREE

MANAGING AND BUDGETING YOUR MONEY

Now that you've started earning money, it's time to learn how to manage it wisely. Earning money is only the first step—what you do with it is what really matters. In this chapter, we'll dive into the basics of budgeting, saving, and spending responsibly. By the end, you'll be able to create a budget, set financial goals, and make smart decisions about your money.

Why Budgeting Matters

Budgeting is all about planning how you'll spend and save your money. Think of it like creating a map for your money, showing where it should go and how much you'll have left. Without a budget, it's easy to overspend and end up without enough money for the things you really need or want. Budgeting helps you stay on track, avoid debt, and reach your financial goals.

When you create a budget, you're taking control of your money instead of letting it control you. It's a skill that many adults struggle with, but learning it now will set you up for financial success in the future.

The Basics of Budgeting

There are three key parts to any budget: income, expenses, and savings. Let's break down each part.

1. Income

Your income is the money you earn. This could be from small jobs, an allowance, or gifts from family members. It's important to keep track of all the money that comes in so you know how much you have to work with each month.

Example: If you earn $50 from babysitting, $20 from doing chores, and receive $30 as a birthday gift, your total income for the month is $100.

2. Expenses

Expenses are the things you spend money on. This could include buying snacks, saving for a big purchase, or donating to a charity. To create a good budget, you need to list all your expenses and group them into categories like entertainment, savings, and gifts.

Example: If you spend $20 on snacks, $10 on a movie, and put $30 into savings, those are your expenses for the month.

3. Savings

Saving is a crucial part of budgeting. You should always set aside a portion of your income for savings. This money can go toward short-term goals, like buying a new game, or long-term goals, like saving for college or a big trip. Building a habit of saving will help you become more financially responsible.

Example: If you save $10 a month, you'll have $120 saved by the end of the year!

How to Create a Simple Budget

Creating a budget doesn't have to be complicated. Here's a simple step-by-step guide to help you get started:

- Step 1: Write Down Your Income

List all the money you expect to receive during the month. Include money from jobs, allowances, or gifts.

Example: $50 from dog walking + $20 from chores = $70 total income.

- Step 2: List Your Expenses

Write down everything you plan to spend money on. Include categories like snacks, entertainment, savings, and anything else you regularly buy. Be honest with yourself about where your money goes!

Example:

Snacks: $15

Entertainment: $10

Savings: $20

Total Expenses: $45

- Step 3: Subtract Your Expenses from Your Income

Once you've listed your income and expenses, subtract your total expenses from your total income to see how much money you'll have left over. If your expenses are higher than your income, you'll need to adjust your spending.

Example: $70 (income) - $45 (expenses) = $25 left over.

- Step 4: Adjust as Needed

If you find that you don't have enough money to cover all your expenses, or you want to save more, you can adjust your budget. Maybe you'll decide to spend less on entertainment or snacks so you can save more. The key is to make sure your income covers your expenses, with some money left over for savings.

- Step 5: Track Your Spending

Once you've created your budget, it's important to track your spending throughout the month to make sure you're sticking to it. You can use a notebook, a spreadsheet, or a budgeting app to keep track of every dollar you spend.

- Setting Financial Goals

A big part of budgeting is setting financial goals. Goals give your money a purpose and help you stay motivated. There are two main types of goals: short-term and long-term.

1. Short-Term Goals

Short-term goals are things you want to achieve in the near future, usually within a few months. This could be saving for a new video game, a concert ticket, or a special gift for a friend. Short-term goals are easier to reach, and they can help you practice good saving habits.

Example: You want to save $60 to buy a new video game in three months. If you save $20 a month, you'll reach your goal in no time!

2. Long-Term Goals

Long-term goals take more time and dedication. These goals might take a year or more to achieve, but they're worth it. Examples include saving for a new computer, a bike, or even starting a college fund. Long-term goals require patience, but with the right budget, you can make them happen.

Example: If you want to save $500 for a new bike over the next year, you'll need to save about $42 a month. It might take longer, but reaching a long-term goal is a big achievement.

The Importance of Needs vs. Wants

When you're budgeting, it's important to understand the difference between needs and wants. Needs are things you must have, like food, clothing, and school supplies. Wants are things that are nice to have, but not essential, like video games, snacks, or movie tickets.

Learning to prioritize your needs over your wants is a key part of managing money. While it's okay to spend money on fun things, it's important to make sure your basic needs are covered first. Once you've taken care of your needs, you can use the rest of your money for wants or savings.

Example: You have $30. You need to buy new school supplies for $15, but you also want to go to the movies with your friends for $12. In this case, you should prioritize buying the supplies first because they're a need. If you have money left over, you can go to the movies later.

Smart Spending Tips

Here are a few tips to help you make smart decisions when it comes to spending your money:

- Think Before You Buy: Before making a purchase, ask yourself if it's something you really need or if it's just a want. If it's a want, consider whether you could save that money instead.

- Look for Deals: Always check for sales, discounts, or coupons before making a purchase. This can help you save money and get more for your budget.

- Avoid Impulse Buying: Impulse buying is when you make a quick decision to buy something without thinking it through. It's easy to fall into this trap, especially when you're shopping online or at the mall. To avoid this, give yourself a day or two to think about the purchase before deciding.

- Track Your Spending: Keep track of where your money goes each week. This will help you stay on budget and spot any areas where you're overspending.

Budgeting might sound boring at first, but it's actually one of the most powerful tools you have to take control of your finances. When you learn how to budget, you're learning how to manage your money in a way that helps you reach your goals, save for the future, and enjoy the things you love.

Remember, it's not about how much money you have, but how you use it. By creating a budget, setting goals, and making smart spending choices, you'll be well on your way to financial success. In the next chapter, we'll dive into the importance of saving and how you can start building a savings habit that will last a lifetime.

CHAPTER FOUR

THE POWER OF SAVING MONEY

Now that you've learned how to budget and manage your money, it's time to focus on one of the most important financial habits you can develop—saving. Saving money is about setting aside part of what you earn for future use. It helps you prepare for unexpected expenses, reach your goals, and build financial security. In this chapter, we'll explore why saving is important, how to set up a savings plan, and the different types of savings accounts available.

Why Saving Matters

Saving money may not sound as exciting as spending it, but it's one of the smartest things you can do for your future. Here's why:

1. Emergencies

Life is unpredictable, and sometimes unexpected expenses pop up—like a broken phone, medical bills, or school supplies you didn't plan for. By having money saved, you're prepared to handle these emergencies without having to borrow money or rely on others.

2. Achieving Goals

Whether you're saving for a new bike, a video game, or a trip with your friends, saving helps you reach your goals faster. It allows you to buy the things you want without having to wait or borrow money. The more you save, the closer you get to reaching your dreams.

3. Building Financial Security

The earlier you start saving, the better prepared you'll be for the future. Having savings gives you financial security and peace of mind, knowing that you can handle unexpected expenses or invest in opportunities as they come along.

How to Develop a Saving Habit

Saving money doesn't happen by accident—it's something you have to plan and commit to. Here are a few tips to help you develop a strong saving habit:

1. Start Small

You don't have to save huge amounts of money right away. Start by setting aside a small portion of what you earn, like 10% or 20%. Even if you only save a few dollars each week, it will add up over time. The important thing is to make saving a regular part of your routine.

Example: If you earn $50 a month, set aside $5 or $10 for savings. After a year, you'll have saved $60 to $120 without even thinking about it!

2. Pay Yourself First

One of the best ways to make sure you save is to "pay yourself first." This means that before you spend any of your money on snacks, entertainment, or other wants, you set aside money for savings. By paying yourself first, you make saving a priority instead of an afterthought.

3. Set Savings Goals

Setting specific savings goals gives your money a purpose. Instead of just saving for the sake of saving, decide what you're saving for and how much you'll need. This will keep you motivated and help you stay focused on your goals.

Example: If you want to save $200 for a new phone, break it down into smaller steps. Save $20 a month for 10 months, and you'll reach your goal!

4. Avoid Temptation

It can be tempting to spend your savings on something fun, especially when you see something you really want. But before dipping into your savings, ask yourself if it's worth it. Is the item more important than your long-term goal? Learning to resist impulse purchases will help you stay on track.

5. Reward Yourself

Saving can sometimes feel like a challenge, so it's important to celebrate your progress. Set mini-rewards for yourself when you reach certain savings milestones. For example, if you save $100, treat yourself to something small like a favorite snack or a day out with friends.

Different Types of Savings

There are different ways to save money, and it's important to choose a method that works for you. Let's look at two main types of savings: short-term and long-term.

1. Short-Term Savings

Short-term savings are for goals you want to achieve in the near future, like buying a game, new shoes, or attending a concert. This money is usually kept in a safe place where you can access it easily when you need it.

Where to Keep Short-Term Savings:

Piggy Bank: If you're just getting started, a piggy bank is a great place to store your short-term savings. You can easily add to it and watch your savings grow.

Cash Envelope System: Divide your money into different envelopes for different goals. Label each envelope with a goal, like "video game" or "new shoes," and put money into it every time you earn.

2. Long-Term Savings

Long-term savings are for bigger goals that take more time to achieve, like saving for college, a car, or a major trip. This money should be kept in a safe place where it can grow over time without being spent.

Where to Keep Long-Term Savings:

Savings Account: A savings account at a bank is a great place to keep your long-term savings. Banks offer interest on savings, meaning your money will grow over time.

Investment Accounts: For even longer-term goals, like saving for college or a house, you can invest your money. Investments involve more risk but have the potential to grow much faster than a regular savings account.

Opening a Savings Account

If you're ready to start saving seriously, opening a savings account at a bank is a great option. A savings account keeps your money safe and pays you interest, which means the bank gives you a little extra money just for keeping your savings there.

1. What You Need to Open an Account

Most banks allow minors to open a savings account with the help of a parent or guardian. You'll need identification, like a birth certificate or passport, and a small amount of money to deposit into your new account.

2. Choosing the Right Bank

When choosing a bank, look for one that offers a good interest rate on savings accounts. The higher the interest rate, the more money your savings will earn. Some banks also offer special accounts for kids and teens that come with extra benefits, like no monthly fees.

3. Tracking Your Savings

Once you have a savings account, you can track your savings online or through a mobile app. This allows you to see how much money you've saved and how much interest you've earned.

How Interest Works

One of the best things about saving money in a bank is earning interest. Interest is extra money the bank pays you for keeping your savings with them. The more you save, the more interest you'll earn.

Example of How Interest Works:

Let's say you have $100 in a savings account that pays 2% interest per year. At the end of the year, you'll have earned $2 in interest, making your total savings $102. The next year, you'll earn interest on the new amount ($102), so your savings will grow even faster.

This is called compound interest, and it's a powerful tool for building wealth over time. The longer you keep your money in a savings account, the more it will grow thanks to compound interest.

Smart Saving Tips

Here are a few tips to help you save more effectively:

Save Automatically: If you have a regular income, set up automatic transfers to your savings account. This way, you won't have to think about saving—it'll happen automatically.

Save Extra Money: Whenever you get extra money, like birthday gifts or holiday cash, put a portion of it into your savings. It's a great way to boost your savings without doing extra work.

Don't Dip Into Savings: Once you've saved money for a specific goal, don't be tempted to spend it on something else. Keep your eyes on the prize and stay focused on your goal.

Challenge Yourself: Set savings challenges for yourself, like saving an extra $5 or $10 each week. Small challenges can make a big difference over time.

Saving is one of the most important financial habits you can develop. Whether you're saving for a short-term goal like a new gadget or for long-term goals like college or a car, the key is to start now and be consistent. The more you save, the more options and opportunities you'll have in the future.

Remember, saving isn't about what you give up today—it's about what you'll gain tomorrow. By building strong saving habits now, you're setting yourself up for financial success in the years to come.

CHAPTER 5

UNDERSTANDING CREDIT AND DEBT

Understanding Credit and Debt

As you continue on your financial journey, it's important to understand two powerful concepts that play a huge role in how we handle money as adults—credit and debt. Credit allows you to borrow money with the promise of paying it back later, while debt is money that you owe. In this chapter, we'll explore what credit is, how debt works, and how to use credit responsibly.

What Is Credit?

Credit is essentially a loan. When you use credit, you're borrowing money from a lender (like a bank or credit card company) with the agreement that you'll pay it back later, usually with interest. It allows you to make purchases or cover expenses even if you don't have the cash at the moment.

For example:

You want to buy a new laptop that costs $500, but you only have $200 saved up. If you have a credit card, you could charge the $500 to your card and pay it off over time.

Types of Credit:

There are different types of credit you might encounter in life, including:

Credit Cards: Credit cards let you borrow money for purchases, but you have to pay it back, usually with interest if you don't pay off the full balance each month.

Loans: This includes student loans, car loans, and personal loans. Loans allow you to borrow a set amount of money and repay it over time with interest.

What Is Debt?

Debt is the amount of money you owe to someone else. Anytime you borrow money and haven't paid it back, you're in debt. Debt can be a loan you took out to buy a car, money you charged on a credit card, or even a loan from a friend.

While debt itself isn't necessarily bad, it can become a problem if you don't manage it responsibly. If you borrow too much or fail to make payments on time, debt can grow quickly and become difficult to repay.

Good Debt vs. Bad Debt:

Good Debt: Some types of debt, like student loans or a mortgage, are considered "good debt" because they help you invest in your future. A student loan, for example, helps you pay for your education, which can lead to a better job.

Bad Debt: This is debt that doesn't offer long-term benefits and often comes with high interest rates. For example, charging unnecessary items to a credit card and failing to pay it off quickly can result in "bad debt."

How Interest Works

Interest is the cost of borrowing money. When you use credit or take out a loan, you usually have to pay back the original amount (the principal) plus interest, which is a percentage of the amount you borrowed. The longer it takes to pay off the debt, the more interest you'll owe.

Example of How Interest Works:

Let's say you borrow $100 and the interest rate is 10%. If you pay back the $100 quickly, you might only owe $10 in interest, making your total payment $110. But if you take a long time to pay it back, you might end up owing much more in interest.

How to Use Credit Responsibly

Using credit wisely is a key skill that will help you avoid falling into debt and protect your financial future. Here are some tips on how to use credit responsibly:

1. Only Borrow What You Can Afford to Repay

One of the biggest mistakes people make is borrowing more than they can afford to pay back. Before you use credit, think carefully about whether you'll be able to repay the money on time. If you're not sure, it's better to wait and save up.

2. Pay Your Bills On Time

Whether it's a credit card bill or a loan payment, always pay your bills on time. Missing a payment can result in late fees and damage your credit score (we'll talk more about credit scores later). Setting up automatic payments or reminders can help you stay on track.

3. Pay More Than the Minimum

Many credit cards and loans require you to make a minimum payment each month. While it might be tempting to only pay the minimum, it's always a good idea to pay more if you can. This will help you pay off your debt faster and reduce the amount of interest you owe.

4. Avoid Impulse Purchases

Credit cards make it easy to buy things you don't need, which can lead to overspending and unnecessary debt. Before making a purchase with credit, ask yourself if it's something you really need and whether you can afford it.

What Is a Credit Score?

A credit score is a number that represents how responsible you are with borrowing money. It's based on your credit history—whether you pay your bills on time, how much debt you have, and how long you've been using credit. Lenders use your credit score to decide whether to lend you money and at what interest rate.

How Your Credit Score Is Calculated:

There are five main factors that determine your credit score:
- Payment History: Do you pay your bills on time?
- Amounts Owed: How much debt do you have?
- Length of Credit History: How long have you been using credit?
- New Credit: Have you applied for new credit recently?
- Types of Credit: Do you have a mix of credit accounts (like credit cards and loans)?

Why Credit Scores Matter:

A good credit score can make it easier to borrow money in the future, whether for buying a car, getting a student loan, or even renting an apartment. A bad credit score, on the other hand, can make it harder to get approved for loans or credit cards and can result in higher interest rates.

The Dangers of Debt

While credit can be helpful when used wisely, it can also be dangerous if not managed properly. Here are some potential pitfalls to avoid:

1. Overspending

Credit cards can make it easy to spend more than you can afford. If you're not careful, it's easy to rack up a lot of debt that you can't pay off.

2. High Interest Rates

If you don't pay off your credit card balance in full each month, the interest can quickly add up. Over time, you may end up paying much more for something than it originally cost.

3. Debt Trap

If you get into the habit of borrowing money and not paying it back on time, you can fall into a debt trap, where your debt keeps growing and it becomes harder to pay off.

Smart Ways to Avoid Debt

Here are a few smart strategies to avoid falling into debt:

1. Stick to a Budget

Creating and sticking to a budget (like you learned in Chapter 3) can help you avoid overspending. Only use credit for things that fit within your budget and avoid using it for impulse purchases.

2. Use Credit for Necessities Only

Try to use credit only for things you need, not for things you want. This will help you avoid unnecessary debt and keep your finances under control.

3. Save for Big Purchases

Instead of using credit to buy big-ticket items, save up for them in advance. This way, you can pay in full and avoid the high interest rates that come with using credit.

Understanding credit and debt is a key part of managing your finances responsibly. Credit can be a useful tool when used wisely, but it can also lead to financial problems if not managed properly. The key is to borrow only what you can afford to repay, pay your bills on time, and avoid unnecessary debt.

.

CHAPTER 6

SMART SPENDING HABITS

After learning the importance of saving money in Chapter 4, it's equally important to know how to spend your money wisely. Spending money is a part of everyday life, but how you choose to spend can greatly impact your financial future. Smart spending habits help you get more out of your money, avoid unnecessary debt, and reach your financial goals faster. In this chapter, we'll explore how to develop smart spending habits and make informed decisions about where your money goes.

Why Smart Spending Matters

Spending wisely doesn't mean never buying the things you want or enjoy—it's about making thoughtful decisions that align with your priorities and goals. When you spend money carelessly or impulsively, it can lead to wasted resources, regret, and even debt. On the other hand, smart spending ensures you get the most value out of your money while staying on track with your financial goals.

Here's why developing good spending habits is important:

Avoiding Waste: Careless spending often leads to buying things you don't need or use, which is essentially wasting money.

Staying in Control: When you have a clear plan for your spending, you're in control of your finances, not the other way around.

Reaching Goals: Smart spending frees up more money to save and invest, helping you reach financial goals faster.

1. Differentiate Between Needs and Wants

One of the most important steps in becoming a smart spender is learning to tell the difference between needs and wants. Needs are the essentials you must have to live, like food, shelter, and transportation. Wants are things you would like to have but can live without, like the latest smartphone, designer clothes, or a fancy meal at a restaurant.

Here's a quick way to determine if something is a need or a want:

Need: Something necessary for survival or daily functioning (e.g., groceries, school supplies, transportation).

Want: Something that makes life more enjoyable but isn't essential (e.g., concert tickets, video games, snacks).

Example:

Need: Buying a pair of shoes because your old ones are worn out.

Want: Buying a new pair of shoes because you like the latest trend, even though your current ones are still in good condition.

When making a purchase, ask yourself: "Is this something I need, or is it just something I want?" Focusing on needs first will help you prioritize your spending and avoid unnecessary purchases.

2. Create a Spending Plan

Just like a budget helps you manage your overall finances, a spending plan helps you stay in control of your day-to-day purchases. A spending plan shows how much you can afford to spend in different categories, like groceries, entertainment, and transportation, while ensuring you still have money left for savings and other goals.

Steps to Create a Spending Plan:
- List Your Income: Write down all sources of income, like allowance, part-time jobs, or gifts.
- List Your Expenses: Write down all the things you need to spend money on each month, like transportation, school supplies, or meals.
- Set Limits: Decide how much you want to spend in each category based on your budget. For example, you might set aside $50 for entertainment and $100 for transportation.
- Track Your Spending: Keep track of your purchases throughout the month to make sure you're sticking to your plan.

By sticking to a spending plan, you'll know exactly where your money is going and avoid the temptation to overspend.

3. Avoid Impulse Buying

Impulse buying happens when you purchase something without planning ahead or thinking it through. It often occurs when you see something you want in the moment and decide to buy it right away. While it might feel good in the moment, impulse buying can quickly drain your savings and leave you with things you don't really need.

Tips to Avoid Impulse Buying:

- Pause Before Buying: When you feel the urge to buy something, take a moment to pause and think. Ask yourself if you really need the item and whether it fits into your budget. Waiting a day or two before making a purchase can help you avoid regret.
- Stick to a Shopping List: When you go shopping, make a list of what you need and stick to it. Avoid adding extra items that aren't on your list.
- Set Spending Limits: Give yourself a limit for how much you can spend on non-essential items each month. Once you reach that limit, avoid buying anything else.

Example:

If you see a cool gadget in the store that you didn't plan to buy, give yourself a day to think about it. If, after 24 hours, you still feel it's worth the purchase and it fits into your budget, go for it. If not, you've saved money!

4. Look for Deals and Discounts

Another smart way to stretch your money further is to look for deals, discounts, and sales. By waiting for the right time to buy or shopping around for the best price, you can get the things you need without overspending.

Ways to Find Deals:

- Sales: Keep an eye out for seasonal sales or discounts at your favorite stores. Many retailers offer big sales during holidays or at the end of the year.
- Coupons: Use coupons and discount codes when shopping online or in stores. Websites and apps like Groupon or Honey can help you find discounts on everyday purchases.
- Buy in Bulk: If there's something you use regularly (like school supplies or snacks), buying in bulk can often save you money in the long run.

5. Spend on Quality, Not Quantity

It's tempting to buy cheaper products to save money, but sometimes spending a little more on quality can save you money in the long run. For example, buying a durable backpack might cost more upfront, but it will last longer and save you from having to replace it frequently.

Example:

Imagine you're deciding between two pairs of shoes. One pair is cheap but made from poor-quality materials, while the other is a bit more expensive but built to last. While the cheaper shoes might save you money now, you'll probably have to replace them soon. The more expensive shoes, on the other hand, will last longer, saving you money over time.

6. Think Long-Term

It's easy to focus on short-term pleasures when spending money, but smart spenders think about the long-term benefits of their purchases.

Before you buy something, consider whether it will still be valuable or useful to you in the future.

Example:
Instead of buying a fast-food meal that you'll eat and forget about, you could save that money and put it toward a long-term goal, like buying a new bike or saving for a trip. Thinking about the long-term can help you make better decisions about how to spend your money.

7. Use Technology to Track Spending
There are many apps and tools available today that can help you track your spending and make sure you're sticking to your budget. These apps can help you see where your money is going and alert you if you're overspending in certain categories.

Popular Spending Tracker Apps:
- **Mint**: Helps you track your spending, set budgets, and manage all your accounts in one place.
- **YNAB (You Need A Budget):** Teaches you how to prioritize your spending and save for future goals.
- **PocketGuard:** Shows you how much money you have available to spend after covering your essentials.

Spending money is a part of life, but how you choose to spend it can make a big difference in your financial future. By learning to distinguish between needs and wants, creating a spending plan, avoiding impulse buying, and looking for deals, you can make your money go further and stay on track with your financial goals.

Smart spending doesn't mean giving up the things you enjoy—it means making thoughtful decisions that help you get the most out of your money. The better you manage your spending now, the more financial freedom you'll have in the future.

CHAPTER 7

THE BASICS OF INVESTING

Now that we've covered saving and smart spending, it's time to explore how you can make your money grow. One of the most effective ways to build wealth over time is through investing. Investing allows you to put your money to work for you, earning returns that can help you achieve long-term financial goals like buying a house, funding your education, or retiring comfortably.

We'll break down the basics of investing, how it works, and how you can start building your financial future through smart investments.

What Is Investing?

At its core, investing is the act of using your money to buy something that you expect will grow in value over time. Instead of simply keeping your money in a savings account, where it earns very little interest, investing allows you to take on a bit more risk in exchange for the possibility of higher returns.

Here's an easy way to think about it:

Saving is for keeping your money safe and earning a little bit of interest. Investing is for growing your money by purchasing assets (like stocks, bonds, or real estate) that increase in value over time.

How Investing Works

When you invest money, you're usually buying an asset that has the potential to increase in value. Over time, as the value of the asset goes up, so does your investment. Of course, there's also a chance the asset could lose value, which is why investing carries more risk than saving.

Types of Investments:
- **Stocks:** When you buy a stock, you're buying a small piece of a company. If the company does well, the value of the stock goes up, and you can sell it for more than you paid. Stocks tend to offer higher returns than other investments, but they're also riskier.

- **Bonds:** When you buy a bond, you're lending money to a company or government. In return, they agree to pay you back with interest. Bonds are generally safer than stocks but offer lower returns.

- **Real Estate**: Investing in real estate means buying property (like a house or land) with the hope that its value will increase over time. Real estate can be a great long-term investment but usually requires a large amount of money to get started.

- **Mutual Funds:** A mutual fund pools money from many investors to buy a mix of stocks, bonds, or other assets. This allows you to invest in a variety of assets without having to choose individual ones yourself.

- **Cryptocurrency:** This is a newer type of investment involving digital currencies like Bitcoin or Ethereum. While some people have made a lot of money investing in cryptocurrency, it's highly volatile and risky, especially for beginners.

Why Invest?

Investing is one of the best ways to build wealth over time. While saving is important for short-term goals or emergencies, the interest earned in a regular savings account is usually very small. Investing, on the other hand, allows you to grow your money more quickly by earning higher returns. The earlier you start investing, the more time your money has to grow, thanks to a powerful concept called compound interest.

The Power of Compound Interest:

Compound interest is what happens when you earn interest not just on the money you've invested, but also on the interest itself. Over time, this can cause your investments to grow much faster.

Example of Compound Interest:

Imagine you invest $100 and earn 5% interest each year. After the first year, you'll have $105. But in the second year, you'll earn 5% on $105, not just the original $100. This means your money grows faster each year, creating a snowball effect.

Risk and Reward: The Balance of Investing

One of the key principles of investing is understanding the relationship between risk and reward. Generally, the higher the potential reward of an investment, the higher the risk. Stocks, for example, can offer big returns but are also more likely to lose value in the short term. On the other hand, bonds are safer but offer lower returns.

Types of Risk:
- **Market Risk:** The risk that the entire market (stocks, bonds, etc.) will go down in value, as can happen during a recession.
- **Inflation Risk:** The risk that the value of money will decrease over time due to inflation, making your returns worth less.
- **Credit Risk**: The risk that the company or government you've lent money to (through a bond) will default and not be able to pay you back.

Balancing Risk and Reward:
When investing, it's important to balance risk and reward based on your financial goals and how much risk you're comfortable with. If you're investing for a goal that's many years away (like retirement), you might be able to take on more risk since you have time to ride out market ups and downs. But if you're investing for a short-term goal, you may want to focus on safer investments.

How to Get Started With Investing

Investing might sound complicated, but you don't need to be a financial expert to start. Thanks to technology, it's easier than ever to begin investing with just a small amount of money.

Steps to Get Started:

Set Your Investment Goals: Before you start investing, think about what you want to achieve. Are you saving for a long-term goal like retirement, or a shorter-term goal like buying a car? Your goals will help determine how much risk you're willing to take.

- Choose an Investment Platform: There are many apps and websites that make investing easy, even for beginners. Popular platforms like Robinhood, Acorns, and Stash allow you to start with just a few dollars.

- Decide How Much to Invest: It's a good idea to start small, especially if you're new to investing. You can always add more money as you become more comfortable. Many experts recommend investing a percentage of your income each month.

- Diversify Your Investments: A key principle of investing is diversification, which means spreading your money across different types of investments (like stocks, bonds, and real estate) to reduce risk. That way, if one investment loses value, your other investments might still grow.

Invest Consistently: Investing regularly over time, rather than all at once, is a smart strategy known as dollar-cost averaging. By investing the same amount of money at regular intervals (such as monthly), you avoid trying to time the market and can benefit from both market highs and lows.

Understanding the Stock Market

The stock market is one of the most well-known ways to invest money. When people talk about investing in stocks, they're usually referring to buying shares of publicly traded companies. The value of these stocks can go up or down based on how well the company is doing and the overall economy.

How Stocks Work:

Shares: When you buy a share of a company, you own a small part of that company. If the company makes a profit, the value of your shares goes up, and you can sell them for more than you paid.

Dividends: Some companies pay a portion of their profits to shareholders in the form of dividends. These payments can provide an additional income stream for investors.

Stock Market Terms:
- Bull Market: A period when stock prices are rising.
- Bear Market: A period when stock prices are falling.
- Portfolio: The collection of all the investments you own.

Common Mistakes to Avoid

While investing can be a great way to build wealth, there are some common mistakes that can cost you money. Here's how to avoid them:

1. Not Starting Early Enough:
The earlier you start investing, the more time your money has to grow through compound interest. Even small investments made early in life can grow significantly over time.

2. Putting All Your Eggs in One Basket:
Investing all your money in one stock or asset can be risky. Diversify your investments to reduce the chances of losing money.

3. Trying to Time the Market:
Many new investors try to buy stocks when prices are low and sell when they're high. But predicting the market is extremely difficult, even for experts. It's better to invest consistently over time rather than trying to guess when the market will go up or down.

4. Letting Emotions Control Your Decisions:
It's easy to get emotional when the stock market rises or falls, but successful investors stay calm and stick to their strategy. Don't let short-term market changes scare you into making impulsive decisions.

CHAPTER 8

CHOOSING THE RIGHT INVESTMENTS

Now that you understand the basics of investing, it's time to dive into how to choose the right investments for your goals. In this chapter, we'll explore different strategies for selecting investments, the importance of diversification, and how to match your investment choices to your personal financial goals and risk tolerance. By the end, you'll have the tools you need to make informed decisions and build a balanced investment portfolio.

What's Your Investment Goal?

Before you begin choosing specific investments, it's essential to know what you're investing for. Different goals call for different investment strategies. Are you investing for a long-term goal like retirement, or do you have a shorter-term goal, such as saving for college or buying a car?

Common Investment Goals:

Short-Term Goals (1-3 years): These goals might include saving for a vacation, a new phone, or a car. Since your timeline is short, it's best to focus on safer investments, such as savings accounts or bonds, that don't fluctuate too much.

Medium-Term Goals (3-10 years): These might include saving for college or buying a home. For these goals, you may want a mix of safe investments and some growth investments (like stocks) to get a balance between security and potential returns.

Long-Term Goals (10+ years): This typically includes retirement or building long-term wealth. Since you have time to ride out market ups and downs, you can invest more aggressively in growth assets like stocks.

Risk Tolerance: How Much Can You Handle?

Every investment comes with some degree of risk, meaning there's always the possibility of losing money. But not all investments carry the same amount of risk. Before choosing investments, it's important to think about how much risk you're willing to take—this is called your risk tolerance.

Types of Risk Tolerance:
- **Conservative:** If you're uncomfortable with losing money or prefer stable, low-risk investments, you have a conservative risk tolerance. You'll likely prefer investments like bonds, savings accounts, and money market funds.
- **Moderate**: If you're willing to take on a little risk for higher returns but still want some security, you have a moderate risk tolerance. A mix of stocks and bonds might suit you best.
- **Aggressive**: If you're comfortable taking on higher risks for the potential of greater rewards, you have an aggressive risk tolerance. You might focus more on stocks, real estate, or even riskier assets like cryptocurrencies.

How to Determine Your Risk Tolerance:

- **Age:** Younger investors can usually afford to take on more risk because they have more time to recover from any losses.
- **Goals:** If you're saving for a short-term goal, you might want to play it safer. But if you're saving for retirement and have decades before you need the money, you can take on more risk.
- **Personality:** Some people are naturally more comfortable with risk, while others may lose sleep when their investments drop in value.

Types of Investment Strategies

There are many different ways to approach investing. Choosing the right strategy depends on your goals, risk tolerance, and how involved you want to be in managing your investments. Here are a few popular strategies:

1. Growth Investing

Growth investing focuses on buying stocks in companies that are expected to grow at a faster rate than the overall market. These companies may not pay dividends, but the idea is that their stock prices will increase significantly over time.

Who It's For: Investors who are willing to take on higher risk in exchange for the potential of higher returns. This strategy is ideal for those with a long-term investment horizon.

2. Income Investing

Income investing involves focusing on investments that generate regular income, such as dividend-paying stocks, bonds, or real estate. The goal is to create a steady income stream, rather than relying on the appreciation of the investment's value.

Who It's For: Investors who want a reliable income from their investments, such as retirees or those with medium-term goals. This is a more conservative strategy compared to growth investing.

3. Value Investing

Value investors look for stocks that they believe are undervalued by the market. These investors try to find companies whose stock prices are lower than their actual worth, with the expectation that the market will eventually recognize the company's value, leading to price growth.

Who It's For: Investors who enjoy doing research and are patient enough to wait for their investments to pay off. This strategy can work well for moderate to aggressive investors.

4. Dollar-Cost Averaging

With dollar-cost averaging, you invest a fixed amount of money at regular intervals (such as monthly), regardless of how the market is performing. This strategy reduces the impact of market volatility because you buy more shares when prices are low and fewer when prices are high.

Who It's For: Investors who want a low-stress approach and don't want to worry about market timing. It's an effective strategy for those who invest regularly, such as contributing to a retirement fund.

Diversification: Don't Put All Your Eggs in One Basket

One of the most important principles of investing is diversification, which means spreading your money across different types of investments to reduce risk. By investing in a mix of assets (such as stocks, bonds, and real estate), you can minimize the impact of a downturn in any one area.

Example of Diversification:
Let's say you invest all your money in the stock of a single company. If that company's stock price drops, you could lose a lot of money. But if you spread your money across different stocks, bonds, and other assets, a decline in one area might be offset by gains in another.

How to Diversify:
Across Asset Classes: Invest in different types of assets, such as stocks, bonds, and real estate, to balance risk and return.

Across Industries: Invest in companies from various sectors (like technology, healthcare, and energy) to reduce the risk of industry-specific downturns.

Geographically: Consider investing in international markets to protect against economic downturns in your home country.

Index Funds and ETFs: Easy Ways to Diversify
If you're not sure where to start with diversifying your portfolio, index funds and ETFs (exchange-traded funds) can be a great option. These funds pool money from many investors to buy a wide variety of assets,

making it easy to diversify without having to pick individual stocks or bonds.

What Is an Index Fund?

An index fund is a type of mutual fund that aims to match the performance of a specific stock market index, such as the S&P 500. By investing in an index fund, you're essentially buying a little piece of all the companies in the index, which helps spread out risk.

What Is an ETF?

An ETF works similarly to an index fund, but it trades on the stock market like a regular stock. ETFs offer flexibility, lower fees, and the ability to buy and sell shares throughout the day.

Who They're For: Both index funds and ETFs are ideal for investors who want to diversify their portfolios without spending a lot of time picking individual investments. They're great options for beginners or those with a moderate risk tolerance.

Review and Adjust Your Portfolio Regularly

Once you've built a portfolio that aligns with your goals and risk tolerance, it's important to review it regularly. Over time, your financial situation and goals may change, so you might need to adjust your investments. Additionally, market changes can affect the balance of your portfolio, and you may need to rebalance to ensure you're still aligned with your strategy.

Steps to Review Your Portfolio:

Check Performance: Look at how your investments are performing compared to your goals. If something isn't performing as expected, it might be time to make a change.

Rebalance: If your portfolio has drifted away from your target allocation (for example, if stocks have grown to make up too much of your portfolio), sell some of the overrepresented assets and buy more of the underrepresented ones.

Stay on Track: Make sure your investment strategy still aligns with your financial goals. If your risk tolerance or timeline changes, adjust your portfolio accordingly.

Choosing the right investments is a personal process that depends on your goals, risk tolerance, and time horizon. By understanding the different types of investments, strategies, and the importance of diversification, you can create a well-balanced portfolio that grows over time while minimizing risk.

CHAPTER 9

AVOIDING COMMON INVESTMENT MISTAKES

Investing is one of the best ways to grow your wealth over time, but it's not without its challenges. Even the most experienced investors can make mistakes that hurt their returns. In this chapter, we'll explore some of the most common mistakes that beginners—and even seasoned investors—make, and how you can avoid them.

1. Trying to Time the Market

One of the biggest mistakes investors make is trying to predict when the stock market will rise or fall. This strategy, known as market timing, involves buying and selling investments based on short-term market fluctuations. The problem? Even professional investors have a hard time consistently timing the market correctly.

Why It's a Problem:

The stock market is unpredictable. If you sell when the market drops, you might miss out on the rebound, when prices start to rise again. Similarly, trying to buy when the market is low can lead to missed opportunities if prices rise faster than expected. Instead of timing the market, a more reliable strategy is to invest consistently over time.

What to Do Instead:

Stick to a long-term investment plan.

Use dollar-cost averaging, which means investing a fixed amount of money at regular intervals, regardless of market conditions.

Focus on your overall financial goals rather than short-term market movements.

2. Letting Emotions Drive Your Decisions

Investing can be emotional. When the market drops, it's tempting to sell your investments to avoid further losses. When the market rises, you might feel the urge to buy more, even at higher prices. But making decisions based on fear or excitement can lead to poor choices.

Why It's a Problem:

Emotional investing often leads to buying high and selling low, which is the opposite of what you want to do. Fear can cause you to sell at a loss during market downturns, and greed can lead you to buy overpriced assets during market bubbles.

What to Do Instead:

Stay calm and remember that market fluctuations are normal.

Stick to your investment strategy, even during market volatility.

Consider automating your investments to remove emotions from the process.

3. Not Diversifying Your Portfolio

We've already talked about the importance of diversification, but it's worth repeating because it's one of the most common mistakes investors make. Putting all your money into one stock, industry, or asset class can be extremely risky.

Why It's a Problem:

If your entire portfolio is tied to one company or sector, you're vulnerable to large losses if that company or sector performs poorly. For example, if you invest all your money in tech stocks and the tech industry crashes, your portfolio could take a significant hit.

What to Do Instead:

Diversify your investments across different asset classes (stocks, bonds, real estate) and industries.

Consider using index funds or ETFs to gain broad exposure to the market.

Regularly review your portfolio to ensure it remains diversified.

4. Ignoring Fees and Expenses

Investment fees and expenses can eat into your returns over time, especially if you're not paying attention to them. Even small fees, when compounded over many years, can significantly reduce the amount of money you earn from your investments.

Why It's a Problem:

High fees can drag down your overall returns, meaning your investments grow more slowly than they could. For example, a fund with a 2% fee might seem small, but over 20 or 30 years, that fee can add up to thousands of dollars in lost returns.

What to Do Instead:

Look for low-cost investment options, such as index funds or ETFs, which typically have lower fees than actively managed funds.

Pay attention to the expense ratios of mutual funds and other investment products.

Avoid frequent trading, as it can lead to higher fees and taxes.

5. Not Having a Plan

Investing without a plan is like driving without a map. You might get somewhere, but it's unlikely to be where you want to go. Many investors start investing without clear goals or a strategy, leading to scattered and inconsistent results.

Why It's a Problem:

Without a clear plan, it's easy to get distracted by the latest trends or market news. You might end up buying investments that don't align with your long-term goals or selling out of fear during market downturns.

What to Do Instead:

Create a clear investment plan based on your financial goals, risk tolerance, and time horizon.

Set specific goals, such as saving for retirement, buying a house, or funding education.

Regularly review your plan and make adjustments as your financial situation changes.

6. Focusing Only on Short-Term Gains

Many new investors get caught up in trying to make quick profits. They may be drawn to "hot" stocks, cryptocurrencies, or other speculative investments in the hopes of getting rich quickly. While it's possible to make short-term gains, it's also possible to lose a lot of money.

Why It's a Problem:

Speculative investments can be very risky and volatile. Chasing quick profits often leads to taking on too much risk and losing money. Additionally, focusing only on short-term gains can distract you from the importance of long-term wealth building.

What to Do Instead:

Focus on long-term growth and wealth accumulation.

Invest in quality assets that have the potential to grow over time, rather than trying to make a quick profit.

Avoid "get-rich-quick" schemes and overly speculative investments.

7. Not Rebalancing Your Portfolio

As the value of your investments changes over time, your portfolio's balance might drift away from your original target. For example, if your stocks perform well, they may grow to represent a larger portion of your portfolio than you intended, increasing your overall risk.

Why It's a Problem:

If you don't rebalance your portfolio, you may end up with too much money in one type of investment, which can expose you to more risk than you're comfortable with. Rebalancing helps you maintain the right mix of investments based on your goals and risk tolerance.

What to Do Instead:

Rebalance your portfolio regularly (at least once a year) to ensure it stays aligned with your target allocation.

Rebalancing involves selling some of the investments that have grown too large and buying more of the investments that have fallen behind.

Many investment platforms offer automatic rebalancing options to help you stay on track.

8. Overreacting to Market Volatility

The stock market goes up and down. Sometimes it can swing wildly in a single day. For new investors, these swings can be scary, leading to overreactions like selling investments during market dips.

Why It's a Problem:

Reacting to short-term market movements often leads to selling low and buying high, which can erode your long-term returns. The best investors understand that market volatility is normal and that it's important to stay the course, even when things seem uncertain.

What to Do Instead:

Focus on the long-term, rather than short-term market movements.

Remember that markets historically recover after downturns.

Avoid checking your investments too frequently if it makes you anxious or tempted to sell.

9. Ignoring Taxes

While taxes are an unavoidable part of investing, many investors don't take them into account when making decisions. Taxes can have a significant impact on your returns, especially if you're frequently buying and selling investments.

Why It's a Problem:

If you sell an investment for a profit, you may owe capital gains tax. Frequent trading can lead to higher tax bills, reducing your overall returns. Additionally, not taking advantage of tax-advantaged accounts, like IRAs or 401(k)s, can mean missing out on tax benefits.

What to Do Instead:

Be aware of the tax implications of your investment decisions.

Hold investments for longer periods to qualify for long-term capital gains tax rates, which are lower than short-term rates.

Maximize contributions to tax-advantaged accounts (like retirement accounts) to reduce your tax liability.

10. Not Starting Early Enough

One of the biggest mistakes young investors make is waiting too long to start investing. Many people think they'll start investing once they have more money, but the truth is, the earlier you start, the better.

Why It's a Problem:

When you start investing late, you miss out on the powerful benefits of compound interest. Compound interest means you earn interest not only on your original investment but also on the interest it has already earned. The longer your money is invested, the more it can grow.

What to Do Instead:

Start investing as early as possible, even if it's with a small amount of money.

Make regular contributions to your investment accounts, even if you can only afford small amounts at first.

Take advantage of compound interest by investing consistently over time.

Conclusion: Stay Focused on the Long Term

Avoiding these common mistakes can help you become a more successful investor and reach your financial goals. Remember, investing is a long-term journey, and the key to success is staying disciplined, avoiding emotional decisions, and sticking to a well-thought-out plan.

CHAPTER 10

TRACKING YOUR PROGRESS AND STAYING MOTIVATED

You've learned how to budget, save, invest, and avoid common financial mistakes. Now it's time to ensure you're staying on track to meet your financial goals. Tracking your progress is crucial to financial success, and staying motivated will help you stick to your plan even when challenges arise.

In this chapter, we'll discuss how to monitor your finances, set realistic milestones, adjust your goals when needed, and keep yourself motivated on your journey toward financial independence.

Why Tracking Your Progress Matters

Tracking your financial progress helps you understand where you stand in relation to your goals. Whether you're saving for a specific goal like college or a car, or building long-term wealth, it's essential to know if you're on track.

Benefits of Tracking Your Progress:

- **Awareness**: It gives you a clear picture of your financial health.
- **Accountability**: Helps keep you accountable to your goals.
- **Motivation**: Seeing progress, even small wins, can motivate you to stay on track.
- **Flexibility**: You can adjust your plan if you're not hitting your targets.

How to Track Your Financial Goals

There are many ways to track your progress, depending on what's most convenient for you. The key is to choose a method that you'll stick with over time.

1. Budgeting Apps

Budgeting apps, like Mint, YNAB (You Need a Budget), or PocketGuard, allow you to track your income, expenses, and savings goals in real time. These apps can help you see how much you're saving, how your investments are growing, and whether you're staying within your budget.

2. Spreadsheets

If you prefer a more hands-on approach, you can create a spreadsheet to track your financial progress. A simple spreadsheet can help you monitor your monthly income, expenses, debt payments, savings, and investment growth.

3. Financial Journals

Some people find it helpful to keep a financial journal where they write down their financial goals, track their spending, and note any progress toward saving or investing goals. This can be a great way to stay engaged with your finances on a daily or weekly basis.

Setting Milestones for Motivation

Breaking down your financial goals into smaller milestones makes them more manageable and helps you stay motivated. These milestones act as stepping stones to your bigger goals, allowing you to celebrate progress along the way.

How to Set Milestones:

- **Short-Term Milestones**: These are achievable within a few months. For example, you might set a goal to save $500 in your emergency fund over three months.
- **Medium-Term Milestones**: These take a bit longer, such as paying off a specific amount of debt or saving $5,000 over the next year.
- **Long-Term Milestones**: These might be several years out, like saving for college or buying a house.

Example:

If your goal is to save $10,000 for a car in three years, break it down into milestones:
- Save $2,000 in the first six months.
- Reach $5,000 by the end of year one.
- Continue adding $2,000 each year until you reach your goal.

Adjusting Your Plan

Life is unpredictable, and sometimes things don't go according to plan. Whether it's a job change, unexpected expenses, or changes in your financial goals, you'll need to be flexible and willing to adjust your financial plan.

When to Adjust Your Plan:
- **Income Changes**: If you get a raise, you may want to save or invest more. If you lose income, you might need to cut back temporarily.
- **Goal Changes**: If your priorities shift (e.g., you decide to go to college instead of buying a car), adjust your savings goals accordingly.

- **Unexpected Expenses**: If you face a major expense like medical bills or home repairs, you might need to pause your savings for a while and refocus your budget.

How to Adjust:
- **Revisit Your Budget**: Update your budget to reflect new income, expenses, or savings goals.
- **Rebalance Your Investments**: If your financial goals have changed, you might need to adjust your investment portfolio to match your new time horizon or risk tolerance.

Staying Motivated

Financial goals, especially long-term ones, require persistence and dedication. It's easy to lose motivation over time, especially when progress feels slow. But staying motivated is key to reaching your financial milestones.

1. Celebrate Small Wins

Every step you take toward your financial goals is worth celebrating. Whether it's reaching a savings milestone, paying off a debt, or hitting a new investment target, acknowledging your progress will help you stay motivated.

2. Visualize Your Goals

One way to stay motivated is to visualize what reaching your goals will feel like. Imagine how it will feel to buy that car, graduate debt-free, or retire early. Keeping the end goal in mind can help you stay focused on the bigger picture.

3. Stay Educated

Continuing to learn about personal finance, investing, and money management can keep you engaged with your financial journey. Read books, listen to podcasts, or follow personal finance blogs to stay inspired.

4. Reward Yourself

Build small rewards into your plan to celebrate your hard work. For example, if you reach a savings goal, treat yourself to something small, like a meal out or a new gadget you've been eyeing. These little rewards can keep you excited about your progress.

5. Find Accountability

Share your financial goals with someone you trust, whether it's a friend, family member, or mentor. Having someone to check in with can help keep you accountable and motivated.

Avoiding Burnout

It's important not to overextend yourself financially. Trying to save every last dollar or putting too much pressure on yourself to meet financial goals can lead to burnout.

Tips to Avoid Burnout:

- **Give Yourself Flexibility**: Don't be too hard on yourself if you fall behind on a goal or encounter unexpected expenses.
- **Set Realistic Goals**: Make sure your goals are achievable based on your income and lifestyle.
- **Take Breaks**: It's okay to pause your savings or investing for a short period if you need to focus on other priorities.

The power of consistency

Ultimately, the key to financial success is consistency. Small, consistent actions—whether it's saving a portion of your income every month, sticking to your budget, or contributing regularly to your investments—add up over time.

Example:

Imagine you invest $100 per month in a stock market index fund that grows at an average annual rate of 7%. After 10 years, your investments will have grown to over $17,000. The power of compounding shows that consistent efforts lead to big results.

CHAPTER 11

THE POWER OF COMPOUND INTEREST

One of the most important concepts in personal finance and investing is **compound interest**. It's often called the "eighth wonder of the world" because of its incredible power to grow your wealth over time. Understanding how compound interest works can help you make smarter financial decisions and set you on the path to financial success.

In this chapter, we'll explore how compound interest works, why it's so powerful, and how you can harness it to grow your money.

What Is Compound Interest?

Compound interest is the interest you earn on both the money you've saved (the principal) and the interest that money has already earned. In other words, it's interest on interest. Over time, this process causes your money to grow at an accelerating rate.

How Compound Interest Works:

1. **Simple Interest**: Imagine you invest $100 and earn 5% interest annually. After one year, you'd have $105. In simple interest, you would earn $5 every year.
2. **Compound Interest**: With compound interest, you earn interest on your original investment plus the interest it has already earned. So, in the second year, instead of earning just $5, you'd earn 5% on $105, which is $5.25. The longer you leave your money invested, the more it grows because each year, you earn interest on a larger amount.

Why Compound Interest Is Powerful

The power of compound interest lies in its ability to turn small, consistent contributions into a large sum of money over time. The earlier you start investing, the more time you have to benefit from compound interest, making it one of the most powerful tools for building wealth.

The "Time" Factor:

One of the key factors that make compound interest so effective is **time**. The longer your money is invested, the more it will grow because each year builds on the previous year's growth. Even small amounts can grow into large sums if given enough time to compound.

Example:

Let's say you invest $1,000 at a 7% annual interest rate. Here's how much it would grow over time:

- After 10 years: $1,967
- After 20 years: $3,869
- After 30 years: $7,612

As you can see, the longer your money is invested, the faster it grows, thanks to the power of compounding.

The Rule of 72

The **Rule of 72** is a quick way to estimate how long it will take for your investment to double, based on the interest rate. To use the Rule of 72, divide 72 by your annual interest rate. The result is the number of years it will take for your money to double.

Example:

If you're earning 8% interest, you can divide 72 by 8 to get 9. This means your money will double in about 9 years.

The Importance of Starting Early

Starting to save and invest early is one of the best things you can do to take advantage of compound interest. Even if you can only save a small amount each month, starting early allows time to work in your favor.

Example:

- **Investor A** starts investing $100 per month at age 20 and stops at age 30.
- **Investor B** starts investing $100 per month at age 30 and continues until age 60.

Assuming both investors earn 7% interest, who do you think ends up with more money at age 60?

- **Investor A**: $168,515
- **Investor B**: $118,590

Even though Investor B contributed for 30 years, Investor A, who only contributed for 10 years, ends up with more money because they started earlier. This is the power of compound interest and time!

How to Maximize the Power of Compound Interest

There are several ways to take full advantage of compound interest and grow your wealth over time.

1. Start Early:

The earlier you start investing, the more time compound interest has to work in your favor. Even if you can only save a small amount, starting young gives you a significant advantage.

2. Be Consistent:

Make regular contributions to your savings or investment accounts. Consistency is key, and even small, regular investments will grow over time.

3. Reinvest Your Earnings:

To maximize the power of compound interest, reinvest any earnings, such as dividends or interest, rather than spending them. This allows your investment to grow even faster.

4. Choose Investments Wisely:

Higher-interest investments, like stocks or mutual funds, have the potential to grow more quickly than lower-interest options like savings accounts. Be mindful of your risk tolerance, but don't be afraid to invest in higher-growth options for long-term goals.

5. Avoid High Fees:

Investment fees can eat into your returns and reduce the power of compounding. Look for low-fee investment options, such as index funds or ETFs, to keep more of your earnings working for you.

The Double-Edged Sword: Compound Interest on Debt

While compound interest can help you grow your savings, it can also work against you when it comes to debt. Many credit cards, loans, and other forms of debt use compound interest to calculate what you owe. This means that the longer you carry a balance, the more interest you'll pay, and the more your debt will grow.

How to Avoid Compound Interest on Debt:

- **Pay off your balance in full each month** to avoid interest charges.

- If you have debt, focus on paying it off as quickly as possible to minimize the amount of interest you pay.
- Avoid taking on high-interest debt, such as credit card debt, unless absolutely necessary.

Compound interest is one of the most powerful tools for building wealth over time. By starting early, investing consistently, and choosing the right investment options, you can harness the power of compounding to grow your savings and achieve your financial goals. Just as importantly, avoiding debt with compound interest will prevent it from working against you.

CHAPTER 12

Budgeting for Tweens – Planning Your Money Wisely

Creating a budget is one of the most important financial skills you can develop, even as a tween. A budget is like a roadmap for your money—it helps you know where your money is coming from, where it's going, and how to manage it so you can reach your financial goals. In this chapter, we'll explore how to make a simple budget, why it's important, and how to stick to it.

What Is a Budget?

A budget is a plan for how you will spend and save your money. It helps you make sure you have enough money to cover the things you need and want, while also saving for future goals. A budget doesn't mean you can't have fun—it just means you're planning ahead so that you can afford everything you want to do.

Why You Need a Budget:

- **Gives control over your money**: You decide how to use your money, rather than wondering where it went.
- **Helps you save**: It ensures you set aside money for future goals, like a new gadget or a special trip.
- **Prevents overspending**: You won't run out of money before the next allowance or payday if you plan wisely.

How to Create a Simple Budget

Budgeting doesn't have to be complicated. Here's a step-by-step guide to creating a budget that works for you.

Step 1: Know Your Income

The first thing you need to figure out is how much money you're bringing in each month. This could be from:

- **Your allowance**
- Money earned from doing chores or part-time jobs
- Gifts or holiday money
- Profits from selling things like crafts or old items
- Write down all your sources of income and add them up. This is your total monthly income.

Step 2: List Your Expenses

Next, write down all the things you spend money on. This can include:

- Fun stuff: Toys, games, apps, movies, or snacks.
- School supplies: Notebooks, pens, or textbooks.
- Activities: Hobbies, sports, or after-school clubs.
- Savings: Money you want to save for something special.

Write down everything you spend money on, even small things. Then, add it up to see how much you spend in a month.

Step 3: Prioritize Your Spending

Now that you know how much you make and how much you spend, it's time to figure out what's most important. You might want to put more money toward savings or cut back on something that isn't a priority.

50/30/20 Rule for Budgeting:

A simple way to organize your budget is to follow the 50/30/20 rule:

50% for needs: Things you really need to buy, like school supplies or food.

30% for wants: Fun things like games, apps, or hobbies.

20% for savings: Money set aside for future goals, like a new bike or a savings account.

If your needs and wants are too high, try to reduce some of your spending in those areas so you can save more.

Step 4: Stick to Your Plan

Once you've made your budget, the most important part is sticking to it. This means you'll have to make choices about where to spend and where to save.

Budgeting Tips for Tweens

Budgeting takes practice, but with a few helpful tips, you can master it and use it to reach your financial goals.

1. Track Your Spending:

One of the easiest ways to stay on budget is to keep track of everything you spend. You can use a notebook, a budgeting app, or even a simple spreadsheet to write down what you spend money on. Review your spending each week to see how well you're sticking to your plan.

2. Save First:

Instead of waiting to see what's left at the end of the month, set aside your savings first. This way, you're sure to meet your savings goals before you spend money on other things.

3. Cut Back on Unnecessary Spending:
If you find yourself spending too much on things that aren't important, consider cutting back. For example, if you're always buying snacks, try bringing food from home instead. Small changes can make a big difference over time.

4. Use the Envelope System:
The envelope system is a fun way to manage your money. Set aside envelopes for each of your spending categories (like fun, savings, and school supplies) and put the money for each category in the right envelope. Once the money is gone from that envelope, you can't spend any more in that category until next month.

5. Review and Adjust:
Your budget isn't set in stone. As your income or expenses change, you can adjust your budget to make sure it still works for you. Review your budget regularly to make sure it's helping you meet your goals.

How Budgeting Helps You Reach Your Goals

One of the best things about budgeting is that it helps you reach your financial goals, whether it's saving for a new game console, planning a trip, or even starting a small business. When you budget, you're making a plan to achieve those goals by setting aside money each month.

Example:
Let's say you want to save up $200 for a new tablet, and you have $50 a month to save. By sticking to your budget and setting aside $50 each month, you'll have enough to buy the tablet in four months.

Budgeting also teaches you discipline, helps you avoid debt, and gives you the confidence to handle bigger financial responsibilities as you grow older.

Mastering Your Money Early
By learning how to budget now, you're setting yourself up for financial success in the future. A budget is more than just a plan—it's a tool that helps you stay in control of your money, avoid unnecessary spending, and achieve your financial goals.

CHAPTER 13

EARNING MONEY AS A TWEEN – START BUILDING YOUR OWN INCOME

As a tween, you're at a great age to start earning your own money. Earning money not only gives you more freedom to buy the things you want but also teaches you valuable lessons about responsibility, hard work, and money management. Whether you want to save up for something special or just have some spending money, there are many ways you can start earning income, even at a young age.

In this chapter, we'll explore creative ideas for earning money, how to turn your skills into cash, and important things to remember when starting your own small ventures.

Why Earning Money as a Tween Is Important

Learning how to earn money while you're young sets the foundation for financial independence. It also teaches you the value of hard work and the importance of managing the money you earn. Here's why earning money as a tween is beneficial:

Builds Responsibility: You learn how to take charge of your time, effort, and financial goals.

Boosts Confidence: Making your own money can make you feel proud and more confident in your abilities.

Encourages Smart Money Habits: When you earn money, you learn how to budget, save, and make better decisions about spending.

Teaches the Value of Work: You begin to appreciate the effort it takes to earn money and spend it more wisely.

Ways to Earn Money as a Tween

There are plenty of ways to make money as a tween, depending on your interests, skills, and opportunities in your community. Here are some ideas to get you started:

1. Chores at Home

Doing extra chores at home is one of the easiest ways to earn money. You could negotiate with your parents to do tasks beyond your usual responsibilities, such as washing the car, organizing the garage, cleaning windows, or doing yard work. Be reliable, and you'll start earning a steady income.

2. Pet Sitting or Dog Walking

If you love animals, offering pet-sitting or dog-walking services could be a fun way to make money. Neighbors or family friends who go on vacation might need someone to take care of their pets. You can also offer to walk dogs in your neighborhood for a small fee.

3. Babysitting

Babysitting is a great way to earn money while helping families in your community. If you enjoy spending time with kids and are responsible, babysitting can be a rewarding way to earn extra cash. Make sure to learn basic babysitting skills and how to handle emergencies.

4. Tutoring

If you're good at school subjects like math, reading, or science, consider offering tutoring services to younger kids or classmates who need help. Tutoring is a great way to earn money while using your academic skills. You can tutor in person or even online.

5. Selling Handmade Crafts

If you're creative, consider making and selling handmade crafts, like bracelets, paintings, or keychains. You can sell your crafts to friends, family, or even set up an online shop with the help of an adult. Crafting allows you to express your creativity while earning money.

6. Yard Work and Gardening

If you enjoy being outdoors, you can offer to help neighbors with yard work. Tasks like mowing lawns, raking leaves, planting flowers, or pulling weeds can be a great way to make money while enjoying the fresh air.

7. Car Washing

A simple but effective way to make money is by washing cars for family, friends, or neighbors. Set up a car wash station in your driveway, and offer to clean cars inside and out. It's a great way to earn some extra cash, especially in the warmer months.

8. Sell Old or Unused Items

Do you have toys, books, clothes, or games that you no longer use? You can sell them online through platforms like eBay or Facebook Marketplace (with the help of an adult), or organize a garage sale. This helps you earn money while clearing out clutter.

9. Start a YouTube Channel or Blog

If you're comfortable with creating content, consider starting a YouTube channel or blog about a topic you're passionate about—whether it's gaming, crafts, or reviewing products. Over time, you can build an audience and potentially earn money through ads or sponsorships.

10. Create Digital Art or Designs

If you're tech-savvy and artistic, you can create digital designs or artwork to sell online. Platforms like Redbubble or Etsy allow you to sell your designs on T-shirts, phone cases, posters, and more. You could also offer graphic design services to people who need logos or other visual content.

Turning Your Skills into Income

The key to earning money as a tween is to think about what skills and hobbies you already have that people would be willing to pay for. Whether it's helping out around the neighborhood or creating something unique, you can turn your talents into opportunities.

Here's how to get started:

Identify Your Strengths: Think about what you're good at—whether it's taking care of pets, organizing, drawing, or coding.

Offer Your Services: Let people know what you're offering by talking to family, friends, neighbors, or posting flyers (with permission). You could also ask for referrals from satisfied customers.

Be Professional: Even though you're young, showing up on time, being polite, and doing a great job will help you build a positive reputation.

Set Fair Prices: Make sure to charge a reasonable amount based on the time and effort required. You can adjust your rates as you gain more experience.

Things to Remember When Earning Money

As you begin to earn money, there are a few important things to keep in mind:

1. Balance Work and School:

School is your number one priority, so make sure you're balancing your work with your studies. Set aside specific times for earning money that don't interfere with your homework, sports, or other activities.

2. Be Safe:

When taking on jobs outside your home, always make sure you have permission from your parents or guardians. If you're working for someone new, have an adult check in to make sure the situation is safe.

3. Keep Track of Earnings:

Once you start earning money, it's a good idea to track how much you make and how much you spend. This will help you see how close you are to reaching your savings goals.

4. Save for the Future:
Remember to set aside part of what you earn for future goals. Just because you have more money doesn't mean you should spend it all right away. By saving regularly, you'll be able to afford bigger things later on.

Starting Your Financial Journey
Earning money as a tween is not only exciting but also a great way to learn important life skills. Whether you choose to start a small business, offer services, or find creative ways to sell things, you're taking the first steps toward financial independence.

CHAPTER 14

SAVING AND INVESTING – GROWING YOUR MONEY FOR THE FUTURE

Now that you've learned how to earn money, it's time to talk about what you can do with that money to make it grow. Saving and investing are two of the most important skills you can develop for long-term financial success. While earning money is important, saving and investing are what help your money multiply over time.

In this chapter, we'll explore the difference between saving and investing, why both are essential, and how you can get started even as a tween.

What Is Saving?

Saving is when you set aside money for future use. It's a way of making sure you have money available for things you might need or want later on, like buying a new bike, going on a trip, or even something big like college.

Why Is Saving Important?

Emergency Fund: Saving helps you prepare for unexpected expenses. What if something you own breaks, or you want to help a friend? Having savings means you're ready for life's surprises.

Big Purchases: If you have your eye on something expensive, like a new gadget or a special event, saving money over time makes it possible to afford it without going into debt.

Building Financial Discipline: Saving teaches you how to manage your money and resist the temptation to spend everything right away.

Tips for Saving Money

Saving money doesn't have to be hard. Here are a few tips to help you get started:

1. Set a Goal

One of the best ways to start saving is by setting a clear goal. Whether you want to save for a new video game, a concert ticket, or your education, knowing exactly what you're saving for will keep you motivated. Write down your goal and how much you need to save.

2. Save First, Spend Later

When you get money from an allowance, a job, or a gift, make it a habit to save part of it right away before you start spending. This way, you won't be tempted to spend everything and forget about your savings goal.

3. Use a Piggy Bank or Savings Account

If you're just starting, using a piggy bank is a fun way to save up cash. However, as you save more, you might want to open a savings account at a bank with the help of a parent or guardian. A savings account keeps your money safe and even earns a little interest.

4. Track Your Progress

Keep a record of how much you're saving each week or month. Watching your savings grow over time can be encouraging and help you stay focused on your goals.

What Is Investing?

Investing is when you use your money to buy something that has the potential to increase in value over time. Unlike saving, where you set money aside and keep it safe, investing involves some risk, but it also has the potential for bigger rewards. The goal of investing is to make your money work for you and grow over the long term.

How Is Investing Different from Saving?

Saving is for short-term goals and emergencies. Your money is kept in a safe place where it won't lose value.

Investing is for long-term goals, like saving for college or your future career. It involves risk because the value of your investments can go up or down, but over time, investing can lead to more significant gains.

Types of Investments for Beginners

Even as a tween, you can start learning about the different ways to invest. Here are a few common types of investments:

1. Savings Accounts with Interest

While not technically an investment, some savings accounts pay interest. Interest is money the bank gives you just for keeping your money in the account. Over time, this can help your savings grow a little.

2. Bonds

A bond is like lending money to a company or the government in exchange for getting your money back later with a little extra. Bonds are considered safer investments than stocks but usually offer smaller returns.

3. Stocks

When you buy stocks, you are buying a small piece of a company. If the company does well, the value of your stocks goes up, and you can make money. However, if the company doesn't do well, the value of your stocks can go down. Stocks are riskier but can offer higher returns over time.

4. Mutual Funds

A mutual fund is a group of stocks or bonds combined into one package. When you invest in a mutual fund, you're investing in many companies at once. This helps spread the risk, making it a safer option than buying individual stocks.

5. Real Estate

Real estate investing involves buying property, like houses or land, with the goal of making money when their value increases. While you might not be ready to buy property now, it's something to think about for the future.

Why Start Investing Early?

One of the biggest benefits of starting to invest when you're young is that you have time on your side. The earlier you start, the more time your investments have to grow. This is thanks to a powerful concept called compound interest.

What Is Compound Interest?

Compound interest is when you earn interest not just on the money you save or invest, but also on the interest you've already earned. It's like earning money on top of money! Over time, compound interest can make your savings or investments grow faster than if you were just adding to it yourself.

Example:

Let's say you invest $100, and it grows by 5% each year. After the first year, you'll have $105. In the second year, you'll earn 5% not just on the original $100, but on the $105. Over time, this extra boost can add up to a lot more money.

How to Start Investing as a Tween

While you may not have access to all the investment options listed above just yet, it's important to start learning and preparing for when you can invest. Here are a few ways to get started:

1. Ask an Adult for Help

Talk to your parents or guardians about opening a savings account or starting a small investment. They can help you understand the basics and guide you through the process.

2. Learn About the Stock Market

Even if you're not ready to buy stocks yet, you can start learning about the stock market by reading books, watching videos, or using stock market simulation apps that let you practice without real money.

3. Invest in Yourself

One of the best investments you can make is in yourself. Learning new skills, reading books, and trying new experiences will help you grow into a smart, capable person who can make informed financial decisions.

The Risks of Investing

It's important to remember that investing always comes with risks. Unlike saving, where your money is safe, investments can go up or down in value. The key is to think long-term and not get discouraged if your investments lose value for a short time. The longer you invest, the more likely your money will grow.

CONCLUSION

Congratulations on completing this journey into the world of financial literacy! You've learned so much—from understanding how to manage money, saving, budgeting, and investing, to borrowing wisely and making smart financial decisions. These are skills that will serve you well throughout your life, helping you build a strong foundation for financial success.

Being financially literate at a young age gives you an incredible advantage. The lessons you've absorbed in this book will guide you in making thoughtful and responsible money choices, setting you up for a future full of opportunities. Here's a recap of some key takeaways to keep in mind:

- **Money is a tool**: Use it wisely by budgeting, saving, and investing to achieve your goals.
- **Set financial goals**: Whether short-term or long-term, having a plan for your money keeps you focused.
- **Be mindful of spending**: Make sure your spending aligns with your values and goals.
- **Save and invest early**: Time is on your side when it comes to growing your wealth.
- **Understand the power of interest**: It can work for you through investments or against you through debt.
- **Use credit responsibly**: Borrow wisely and always aim to pay off debt quickly to avoid costly interest.

By mastering these skills, you're already on your way to financial independence and security. The world of money can sometimes seem complicated, but with the knowledge you've gained, you have the tools to navigate it confidently.

Remember, financial literacy is a lifelong journey. As you grow, so will your understanding of money, and that's okay. Continue learning, asking questions, and making informed decisions. The better you manage your money today, the brighter your future will be tomorrow.

www.ingramcontent.com/pod-product-compliance
Lightning Source LLC
Chambersburg PA
CBHW050319230526
45471CB00005B/2261